Things To Do Before You Leave Town

Ross Sutherland was born in Edinburgh in 1979. A former lecturer in electronic literature at Liverpool John Moore's University, Ross works as a freelance journalist and tutor in creative writing. This is his first collection.

Things To Do Before You Leave Town

Ross Sutherland

penned in the margins

PUBLISHED BY PENNED IN THE MARGINS
53 Arcadia Court, 45 Old Castle Street, London E1 7NY
www.pennedinthemargins.co.uk

First published 2009

Printed in Great Britain by the MPG Books Group, Bodmin and King's Lynn

ISBN
0-9553846-4-8
978-0-9553846-4-6

*To my parents
and my grandparents*

CONTENTS

ACKNOWLEDGEMENTS

Acknowledgements are due to the following publications and programmes: Bespoken Word (BBC Radio 4), *The Fix*, *Live From The Hellfire Club*, *Reactions*, *Rising*, *Tears in the Fence*.

A number of these poems were written for and first performed in the following live literature productions: Powerpoint (Aisle16), Poetry Boyband (Aisle16), Services to Poetry (Aisle16), Found in Translation. 'By The Time You Read This, I Will Be In Switzerland' was commissioned by Nabokov for Present : Tense.

~

Thanks to the hundreds of people every year that wake up to find me on their sofa.

Special thanks to Tom Chivers, Joe Dunthorne, Chris Hicks, Luke Wright, Tim Clare, Nafe Jones, Nick Holloway, Dave Bamford, Mo Herdman, Joel Stickley, Gary Dylan Seal, Kevin Murphy, John Osborne, John Smith, Kieran Hood.

Things To Do Before You Leave Town

All the best

Bitches always come back

GRETL VON TRAPP

The Message

A musical sculpture has been installed
inside a pitch black gallery.
The song contains a hidden message
oscillating between the notes,
like tapes found under pillows,
spooling advice into not-too-distant futures.

"What does it say?" I ask the artist.
On the other end of the phone there is a whining sound
like overloaded dumb waiters.
The artist evades the question. "It says the same thing,
over and over and over," he deadpans. "Hmmm," I say.
Mistaking this for a dialling tone, the artist hangs up.

It is always the same young gallery assistant
I find clacking her heels against the stool.
I reason no one has heard the sculpture more times than her.
Each time I leave the darkened room
I ask her what she thinks the message is.
Her eyes roll back as if reading it off the rafters:

"Entertainment is a medical reaction."
"Better the scorpion you don't know."
"Art is filibusting in the abyss."
"I still hate Thatcher."
"There may be safety in numbers, but no dignity in the data."
"Everywhere we go, people are bastards."

We know we're getting closer every day.
I bring her cans of Coke and fan her with my programme.

"Pastiche cumulo-paroxysms," she says,
the words turning over in her mouth like information.
The art has encoded itself into her posture,
the message blurring on her lips as she sleeps.

The final time I visit, the room is bright.
The gallery assistant is sitting in the middle
of a fluorescent mechanical quilt. She is flanked
on both sides by skeletons in symmetrical Fonzie stances.
She looks sheepish, as if she has lured me
into some horrible trap set by the artist.

I expect the apocalypse to go something like this.

Things To Do Before You Leave Town

Attempt to tessellate everything
you've never wanted
and ever known.
Cut the phone. Bleed the radiators.
Cancel bills, subscriptions, friendships.
Tell Steve to go fuck himself.
Introduce your creditors
to those who owe you favours.
Find something creepy
to offer your neighbours:
a small key, a stethoscope.
I thought you might like this...
Use 'mate' like a newsagent.
Meet Claire, but fail to notice.
Do not set out a timetable of withdrawal.
Do not return your library books.
Do not go back for your coat.
Do not hard-talk the homeless.
Do not stare longingly up at the clock tower.
Stop taking yourself so seriously.
This is your final warning.
Put on 'Uptown Top Rankin'
in the first pub you drank in.
Try to enjoy the boredom.
If you can, spread it around.
Come midnight, throw
a glow-in-the-dark frisbee
off the highest point in town.

Jean-Claude Van Damme

My dad hijacks a nuclear warhead
and threatens to launch it
at the Statue of Liberty
if his demands are not met.

He salutes a wall of televisions;
sallow-skinned agents are activated in Honduras,
followed by Washington, Rome, Peru,
each with a briefcase handcuffed to their wrist

and a scorpion tattooed on one buttock.
Codes are scrambled. Intelligence suggests.
Manic laughter brings down a chopper, whilst
fresh ammunition is shuttled to the coast.

Dad puts a bullet through his general's eye.
There are reports of a life-sign *inside the perimeter*.
Guards are found naked or not at all.
Torture chambers flood with blood.

The adventure ends. His army crushed,
my father stands alone on his secret island,
staring into broken radar screens, sparks
raining off his trim, well-decorated uniform.

I pause the video less than a second before
Jean-Claude Van Damme rolls out the darkness,
then edge the film on, frame by frame,
until the image closes in like hands around a neck

and my dad's eyes dilate for the last time,
lips dribbling scarlet plasma.

Then I get down on my hands and knees,
bring my face up to the television set

and tell him that sometimes it's OK to lose.

The Family Blessing

Ten years old, jammed into a Dolomite Sprint,
my Ant Hill cousins are in matching suits,
monobrows hovering fiercely above the parcel shelf;
four in the back, one in the trunk.

I gun the car towards the church, topiary skidding
past us like a backlog of severed thumbs.
At the wedding, the boys give a cryptic blessing,
mouths bursting with popping candy.

"They are saints," says Aunt Tina.
A car back-fires somewhere beyond the tombstones.
I think of their immaculate bedrooms and inscrutable
holiday photos. The oath of silence that galvanises

small acts of violence: shredded shoulders,
Lynx flamethrowers, the odd bloody handprint.
Sammy Pockets and Ice Cream Benj are hitting up Dad for cash.
John The Square cases the perimeter, while Dougy

sticks his gum under the table for later.
Babyface Sutherland jams my car keys into the small of my back
and I can hear his mouth fizzing like a detuned radio,
making me an offer I can't refuse.

My Curse

I am a *gobshite*, specifically so.
Officially registered with my butter and my windmills
and the clack clack clack of my bloody go-ons,

and proud I am too.
For we have built an unparalleled classification system;
a codebook of curses as articulate as the saints.

For we know that a *tosser* is a level-two *wanker*,
can tell a *chav* from a *ned* from the cut of his headrests.
We know that *dickheads* are predominantly girls
and that *arsewipes* are *arseholes* without portfolio.
That *cunt* trumps a *bastard* and would cross town to do so.
That *gits* know they are, but *twats* (oh, sad *twats*) do not.

But spare a thought for the lesser-spotted:
the *dunderheads* and *divvys*, all but wiped out;
benders and *gaylords*, forced to convert in that historic 1988 amnesty,
while *uphill gardeners* ploughed secretly away,
their employers unaware they were even swearing.

We are down to fewer than fifty *cumsocks*,
now found solely outside motorway services,
kicking at the swings.

                    And I can guarantee
you have seen your last *wazzock*, my friends.
Like a huge unblinking question mark standing in your driveway.
Toys boxed in the attic. The last itchy chin.

When Paperboys Roamed the Earth

Your scrappy Reeboks are the first to break the frost;
a bicycle track surgically stitching our hollow streets together.
And nobody knows these bungalows better.
Each detail of our back gardens: the debris of playthings;
hoarded bricks that refused to be barbecues;
ripped cans and wet ashtrays.
Picking past croquet hoops and dog shit,
you navigate our traps
to pass daily judgement on our novelty doormats.

From the daily exchange at our letterbox,
it seems you have become a connoisseur of us.
You know when our children have brought home a fuck,
how the widowers smell different from the divorcees,
the death of a goldfish instantly broadcast
by the condensation on our toilet windows.

Your satchel maps our pavement politics,
exposing a secret vein of *Times* readers,
shifting into salmon as the fences rise.
Blotches of red-tops fester in cul-de-sacs;
both a *Guardian* and a *Sun* for the Fitzpatricks at 12,
their conversation like tectonic plates across the breakfast bar.

Next door, J. Bruce stuffs yesterday's *Mail* into sodden brogues,
property pages retained for the post-Evensong massacre of spiders.

Smoke rises from the scrub. The telegraph poles
end here— this is as far as word can travel.
Back in bed, you compile your report in dreams.

Dogs bark instructions at the moon.
Polished umber cars are unlocked at a distance.
Men with windy faces watch ducks raping ducks
on recently reshingled driveways
as Tuesday arrives. A thousand bald patches begin to itch.
An egg boils. Here is the news.

Funeral Song

We look fit at funerals, you and I.
As we file past the casket, bow and turn,
your black veil flares, my gothic perm
caught in the reflection of a platinum urn
lit by candles. The soft focus of tears
that keeps us looking so young and fresh.
The immaculate cut of my suit, your dress,
against the chessboard of cousins and colleagues.

The sweet ache of monochrome that swerves hearts
like magnets. (Come my love, Man Ray would get it—
take a cursory glance at the history of aesthetics.
How Rauschenberg the sky is; how Riley our eyes;
how it took Chanel to give Death a tie.)
A mathematics of line and shade
that would imbue the most pitiful holiday snap
with the jouissance of the French New Wave.

Let us call it Kansas, back where it all began.
(And you were there. And you. And you.)
Let us walk like the Rat Pack, coffin aloft,
with the best dressed member sealed in the box.
Let's call for Makeup, for that touch of continuity.
Our script, film noir; some classic remade,
and nothing is more classically designed than a grave.

Black and white is a durable idiom,
immortality a blessing as well as a curse.
Some things never go out of fashion:
the camera, the pupil, the inkwell, the hearse.

Logon

1.

I remember visiting your office as a child.
The constant hum of hard terminology.

You at your desk in a polyester coat,
surrounded by coffee and post-dated post-its.

We tailgated through tunnels, alphanumeric airlocks,
past rows of murmuring units. Chain-smoking deputies

sat at their terminals, glowing like thrones,
their Martian fingers sliding beneath the city.

You with one hand against the window.
The smell of paper on your shoulder.

I was your pink biodegradable robot.
My name, your secret password.

2.

Your name was our secret password.
Hating you unconditionally from the age of six,

we made you the entry code to our den,
a woodland shambles where we planned minor atrocities,

swapped nosebleeds for the synopses of horror films, blocked out
the summer, exchanged your name for a stretch of darkness.

Later reprised when cornered by police, though sometimes we
would forget that only one of us could be you on any given arrest.

Once I claimed to be the guy standing next to me.
He then claimed to be me out of spite.

That night we dropped a breezeblock on the hideout,
pretending that you were still trapped inside.

3.

Usually names of girls I fancy, which I am obliged
to update every month. I try not to be too obvious,

burning the trail as I go. This way, I dispense
with the knife and the tree. I save face and xylem.

Sometimes I find it written on my hand, or in the top right
corner of my diary. To my friends I'm

the great firewall of China. On strangers
I barely ever use protection.

Having been hacked since before I was born,
can you be sure who's behind those eyes,

shoulder-surfing for those opening keystrokes
as I stoop to kiss your neck?

Autopsy

Obituaries from Yassir Arafat, John Peel, Old Dirty Bastard, Emlyn
Hughes (November, 2004)

Balding, paunchy and badly dressed, he had the air of
a Philadelphia McDonald's parking lot,
wearing a cheeky grin
and a pistol, born for so long on his hip, that
rap music evolved around him.
He could claim to have broken The Fall and
the White House lawn.

His first marriage to a 15-year-old Texan girl was dissolved
into 20 vials of crack — like
a plane crash,
pre-recorded, and broadcast every night
for the last ten years.

He was later arrested for failure to pay child support
and announced that he enjoyed "vigorously grand-
parenting"
with a "face of terror."
His nasal pronunciation and short vowel sounds were
powerfully
derailed by persistent violence.

Determined to restore Palestine to the roadmap
he became a DJ in Dallas
and played songs that sounded like people fighting —
a style that earned him the nickname *Crazy Horse.*
But despite the hallucinogenic overtones, he refrained from

indulging in
    corruption, misrule and human rights abuses,
as he led his wolves directly into
    the hearts of suspicious teenage listeners.

He signed interim peace accords with Israeli leaders Yitzhak Rabin
and Shimon Peres,
    appearing together on a Mariah Carey remix.
Clearly not on the payroll of any record company, his words carried
weight.

    With the onslaught of Beatlemania
he was shot in the back and arm
    by Liverpool boss Bill Shankly
but the wounds were superficial.

Living at his mother's home under house arrest,
    he was somehow enduringly adolescent and old before his
time,
a modern day
    television quiz show
phoenix,
    who installed a one-party system
but could play in three different positions,
    a spirit of the all-conquering Liverpool side
with boundless reserves of drive, enthusiasm and battling qualities,
    who vowed to
play The Sex Pistols' "Anarchy in The U.K."
    until his country was united.

Death is
    an eclectic programme,
anchored off the North Sea,
        frightening in its intensity,

not afraid to put an arm around a princess,
       survived
only by its own
       statelessness,
rife with cronyism, run so single-handedly that even
       after 40 attempts on his life, his
autobiography remained incomplete;

       an occupied territory, full of
after-dinner speakers and
       the impenetrable free-form rhymes
of a heart attack in October.
       A four-man underground cell
on an endlessly airborne routine.

Invitation to a Search Party

Hey. My house is empty —
why don't we have a search party?

It will be *the social event of the season*
and will probably last for days.
        And who isn't a fan
of those timeless search-party games???

First searching for reasons, then for words,
then light switches, solace.
        Everyone's invited,
and no police, I promise.

So spread out guys; link hands girls.
This is a caper in reverse.
Not a social gathering
        but a social dispersal —

heading out from a single point,
flattening fields in moonlight,
dragging the lake with hardened eyes,
        hollering names into woodland.

Til the party forgets
what it's searching for
        or what the morning
was supposed to deliver.

While I, the absent host, sleep on —
my daring breakout, dragged downriver.

Critical Praise for My Last Relationship

At first glance, our faces appeared little more
than frayed notes, hinting at a distant mood.
Yet, on reflection, there was something compelling in that fraying.
My beard was loaded with the channeled pressure of speech.
Her eyes were not one thought, but two.

Each day we spent together had a distinct tone and shape.
Our subject range was impressive:
a man talks through his previously owned automobiles;
a snowflake flowers upon a petri dish;
Ovid laments his exile from Rome.

In winter, we underwent an odd shift of register.
Humour masked an aposiopesis. I trailed off into Northern Slang.
My invocation of a lost England was haunting in its fragility,
a place Frank Ormsby at *The Belfast Telegraph*
described as 'a world of cries'.

She was as personal as Emily Dickinson. I was as striking.
We were happy spanning joy and death together,
cutting out every word we dared,
walking out onto empty streets,
heat rising up into the negative space above us.

There were occasional poor lines,
but they were made noticeable by their rarity.
A meditation on the exchange of Christmas gifts,
whilst well written, felt too much
like a generic picture of despair.

Scotch Corner

Dawn lies motionless on the silted staff-room carpet
as sunlight spills across from Yarm to bleach the indoor market.
And with the sun, the A1 coughs a fleet of empty faces.
Each limp distinctive, yet their bladders make them natives.
They come to smack their children and try to keep the bins clean,
memory of departure sharper than a sparrow through the
       windscreen.
A nicotine-stained ceiling weighs on her piece-rate heart.
Dawn dreams of Darlington, the fire-door ajar.

Guarded by the shy fluorescence of the AA representative,
a lady blows her coffee cold, the lucky dip claw tentative.
Cut from polyester, legs pale beneath the tanning,
sheer sheer professionalism: half dreading, half planning,
as chastened wit in stencilled script hilariously looms,
an ancient curse: *I have measured out my life in coffee spoons…*
On the other side, Dawn smoothes her eyes, then reapplies the
       rouge
as tanker after tanker succumbs to centrifuge.

Sheila jams the porter filter back in the machine,
left hand angling the milk til the meniscus screams.
"Dawn passed out in the staff-room," she says to Karen behind her.
The blue plaster on her eyebrow dips. She kills the coffee grinder,
goes to stack the plastic cups and collapse a box,
then returns to the fridges to date-rotate the stocks.
Sheila consults the register, then turns to the gentleman facing:
"I've just got to switch the till roll over, sorry to keep you waiting."

Casino Exit

He stands, and it starts
with the valet's alarum.
For one second, time is noticeable by its absence.
His adversaries stack their remaining chips
into new democratic assemblies,
yellow fingers clashing on the purple felt.
This is the only window he needs.

Half man, half Bellagio hair-gel,
the deserter flips a chip to the croupier
then vanishes, sideways,
into a group of off-duty Laotian kitchen hands.
The casino grins, vestibules
swarming with garrulous fruit machines.
Men in pink waistcoats play eye-tennis across the pit.
Hypno-carpets are cranked from 'arouse' to 'baffle'.
Yet somehow our man is already jogging through the mezzanine,
burning the trail as he goes,
kicking his shoes down an empty lift shaft,
a champagne cork neatly masking a fart.

The croupier opens his hand —
a chocolate doubloon. And it's not even Christmas.
He powders it into a mirrored ashtray.

There are sightings of a man disguised
as a disaffected kitchen porter,
taking a shortcut through a water feature.
Tuxedoed thugs cram into the stairwell,
popping a child's balloon with a cocktail stick as they pass.

"He's ours. He's ours," they yell over their shoulders.
"Ours, ours, ours," echoes the man,
following them to the stockroom door.

The casino sends their Blade Runner up to the roof.
A soliloquy is made about risk versus reward,
weather systems falling around him.

Our hero limps through corkscrewing corridors,
neon autographs burnt onto the backs of his eyes.
From here on out, all doors must be buzzkilled open.
Each has the generic voice of a local radio presenter.
"What's brown and sticky?" asks the door.
"Coastal wetlands," he replies. The door succumbs.
"Why did the pony cough?" asks the next.
"Probably some sort of obstructive pulmonary disorder."

Men with gloves convene in the Sky Lounge.
The Blade Runner is giving a slideshow.
The men are dying. Their eyes appear to be drawn on.
A sweaty lieutenant intrudes: *Sir, we found his hat
on a polystyrene Tanuki, but he's gone!*

What can the pit boss do but push buttons?
Look— there he goes,
emerging from under an opera singer's dress.
He's cleared the perilous spiral staircase;
the lobby sways, no trap-doors, and OUT,
out across the empty car park
under a cosmos of shorted fibre optics,
leaving the odds crippled on the bank of an accelerated estuary,
a black speedboat, seen only by the glitter of its wake.

Two Moons for Mongs

Frosty mongs bosh shots of Scotch
on London's Brook Common,
rock-off to soppy mono toss;
lost songs of London:
Town of Bop.

No motor. No lolly. No job to mock.
From tons of pot
down to Jon's bong only
(too strong for Tony,
only Tony don't know so).

Gordon's cold brown cosh
of old hotdog
now looks *so good.*
Tony scoffs lot; sods off
to look for Polos.

Johnny shows Gordon how to body-pop:
slow Robocop foxtrot
to Bobby Brown.
Scot robs Holly's shock blowjob story;
lots of ho ho ho follows.

Two o'clock:
Tony growls *bon mot* bollocks
from London's soft throng of woods;
lost moth for God's two moons.
Poor Tony looks down, drops
Pollock on both boots.

On plots so holy,
old dogs poo boldly.
Goons do loops of blocks,
too cold for words.

Gordy pops bon bons.
Jon spots...

Bono.

Both gobs go
'O'.

The Three Stigmata of Pac-Man

1.

Walls

If you get high enough, any city looks pretty,
but only Home glows blue at dawn,
when an old man with an endless yawn
can make his own constellations in the streetlights.

He traces the high-rise concrete shelves;
each backstreet, a sheet of braille.
A broken telegram from God, he thinks;
orders sluicing through neon gutters

and he'll follow them,
doggedly.
He'll thirstily drain it.

For there is something timeless between the buildings here.
Some classic design that can never be updated.

2.

Ghosts

Spurred by the sirens, he remembers the orphanage:
the pale curtains with the bleeding heart motif;
the first taste of communion in his hollow jaw;
the bed, no bigger than a cake tin.

He remembers his mother — golden, complete —
as if looking up from the bottom of a well,
an emergency sunset on an unknown horizon;
and a tear runs from his one eye.

These nightmares have become his shepherds;
nightly visitations of past, future and present
with lessons demanding endless restlessness.
It suits the strange name the children gave him—

this endless craving of virgin pavement.
Deep ruts, cut in search of safe haven,
thirty years deep, yet still need engraving.
These *ghosts* have somehow found a way in,

of keeping him moving, quickly, silently,
doubling back across empty streets.

3.

Pills

Every town has its cold, hard edges;
unfamiliar estates, laced with narcosis.
Luck changing in sharp winds, stinking of sulphur.
Roads with sadder stories to tell.

But out here, the janitor is Minotaur.
An amphetamine pumping his broken heart.
A hunger for time itself,
as if the very word could be swallowed.

And for one brief moment, every road leads home:
the city becomes a lover's face,
an old film he can mouth every word of,
a Bible passage beaten into him backwards,

a suit, worn every day til retirement,
the pen still expectant in the inside pocket.
For one second, there is nothing to run from,
for who can feel loneliness inside the womb that bore them,

when all the roads that lead out are really leading back in?
No discontentment can exist without a star to wish upon.
And so he sleeps — he does not know for how long, just
long enough to forget what he has to.

That night, the future called out to him in dreams.
It looked exactly the same, only slightly faster.

By The Time You Read This, I Will Be In Switzerland

"Tourists come at lunchtime and by the afternoon they are dead."
Dorle Vallender, Swiss Parliament

There have been so many corridors
and taxi drivers and ears and fees
and men from White Knight Insurance,
but now comes the time —
now, as the seatbelts fasten, the Alps gouging the cloud cover.
Now all that remains of the world is Zurich.

Home to the biggest clock-face in Europe!
Home to black truffles, bittersweet and peaceful evenings.
Home to Tina Turner for the last nineteen years,
where gentlemen sit down to pee between 10 and 6am. It is *heaven*!

It's the kind of place where you stop for a day and stay forever,
says Joe Ritchie, American entrepreneur
who lives in Geneva but visits Zurich often.
Litter doesn't seem to even touch the ground.

We buy matching Cabaret Voltaire
limited-edition Swatch watches (70 francs).
On the strap, a quote from Kurt Schwitters:
Immortality is Not Everybody's Thing.

Down in the hotel's Da-Bar,
tourists listen back to a recording of Hugo Ball,
cheering when he is manhandled off-stage,
lost in a maze of his own irony.

In our room, the chairs are nailed to the ceiling.
We sit on the bed and watch some TV,
a dubbed transmission of *The Fresh Prince of Bel-Air*.
Uncle Phil dissolves into illogical phonetics.

Across town, twelve Giacometti statues
are carefully positioned to avoid each other's eye contact.
Old men play giant chess
amongst the trees in Lindenhof Square.

At seven, the lobster rings.
Apparently, our longing for death
has been sufficiently consistent for the authorities.
We have an address in Kilchberg and a time.

There is a coffee machine and some champagne glasses
and a collection of walking sticks
which we're welcome to add to.
We're seriously advised not to arrive early.

A woman in the lobby informs us
of a performance of Stravinsky's
Rite of Spring this evening.
But we don't go.

For dinner we have veal steak
accompanied by sautéed vegetables and galettes.
A dessert of rhubarb and strawberry charlotte.

The School Counsellor

A bowie knife is jammed into a schoolboy's back,
dug in, then yanked, his jumper half-hoisted.

The boy acts like he's in on the joke.
He forces a chuckle, chalky bubbles on his shuddering lips.
His friends point out the urine stain appreciatively.

It is lunchtime. Sensing the bell, he pulls his weight
onto the picnic table, makes a joke
about having to buy a new shirt anyway,
then looks around the playground
for someone less liked than he is.

He sticks his tongue out of the corner of his mouth
and rolls back his eyes,
mocking the dead with all his strength
as his clothes fill up with blood.

~

In afternoon lesson, the kids watch rapt as Mrs Boil
gibbers her way through Roman armaments,
violently switching into auxiliary verbs, then photosynthesis,
an obbligato on the cost of replacing fine-liners,
ending on a screech of minibeasts
as she climbs into the Wendy house
and blows her shattered brain out.

~

The headmaster's corridor displays monochrome
nightmares of a bygone era: kids
walking into the wrong changing rooms
or trapped inside unfathomable climbing frames.
There is a montage of children
who have arrived without their trousers,
all grown-up by now, one guesses;
each one of them with kids of their own,
sleepwalking their way to the top of the stairs.

Something Detonates

We woke to the sound of one hand clapping.
Sudden, black and acrid, a question mark
rose above the numerical terraces.
From the window we watched a dog do the ouroboros,
like a record with the needle in its final groove.

With no clues, we meditated for a while.
It's impossible to know when Buddha
is cracking a joke these days – such a dry arse.
We sent out Donald as a makeshift probe.
He came back with a suntan, drunk on Existentialism.

On the front of his newspaper, through a pixel veil,
we saw the deadly brainteaser for ourselves,
discharging endless multiple choices
onto the smouldering tarmac, while the caption
ran optimistically through interrogative pronouns.

At the blast radius, simpler questions
were being turned over, after the states
of relatives and the reliability of numbers.
It was all very Socratic, mums locked into lilting dialogue
under the shadows of the avenued poplars.

The earth itself felt wanting, asking us if we smoked.
We took out our fags and crushed them in.
By now the fallout had drifted far beyond the cities.
Even my mother, out in the Hebrides,
began to interrogate her flock.
Word came of roaming, thousand-strong chat shows.

Canned responses became untenable.
We gathered around the television, warming our eyes,
until the final flakes of raw static fell.
You appeared in a coat made from National Geographics.
I fashioned a gun from a Smartie tube,

popped the lid, then locked myself in the cellar.
It appears our drunken quizmaster, learned though he is,
never got around to finishing what he started.
First the radio, looping *What's Going On?*
Then me, thanking the darkness.

Nephelococcygia

Before undertaking anything, whether
a business transaction, a conversation, or the purchase of food,
I consult the planes.

When the visibility is good
and the flight paths are in alignment
I will put in a call. Come midnight
you will be walking purposefully
through the departure lounge of Roissy,
one of you across the floor, one across the glass ceiling,
hair unpacked, on your way back home.

I try to think of the sky as a country unto itself;
one of which only a privileged few have citizenship.
You, beneath felt beret and regulation eye makeup,
adjusting headrests, counseling those not ready to go,
shepherding the prayers of the business class.

This is your republic. A house of cards, maybe,
but I believe in it.

I leave small sacrifices at the horizon;
throwing in a boomerang as the sun goes pink.
I send up kites, searching for cracks in gravity,
then try to wedge myself through the ramparts.
I time my blinks with yours
then make names for the constellations I see:
The Nail Bomb, The Airbag, The Hydrocarbon;
the shapes floating apart, towards
distant control towers that I can barely imagine.

These things are good omens:
      items found in high, unexpected places;
      old newspapers on top of wardrobes;
      shoes on roofs;
      families of acrobats;
      giant Toblerone.

These things are bad omens:
      Blue Peter Annuals;
      log cabins;
      vortexes;
      anything by Big Bopper, Patsy Klein, John Denver.

Relations between earth and sky have always been uneasy
and I try my hardest to know this, as I switch on the TV
at your breathless request from a Novotel in Venice.
Your tiny voice tells me that no seat is safer than any other.
Even mine, back here on Earth. Yet this is the closest I have ever got
to weightlessness, watching firemen pick through the wreckage
towards a man still strapped into his seat,
hands in flames, as if he held a thunderbolt.

No last words on the black box recorder
bar the PA's automated mantra:

Put out your cigarette, this is an emergency descent.
Put out your cigarette, this is an emergency descent.
Put out your cigarette, this is an emergency descent.

If Hitler

"If Hitler was alive today he would be the toast
of every bioethics committee," I say.
"He would have fingers in Ofcom and the face of abortion,
and on Sundays he would play golf with Chomsky."

The room falls silent. "And he would win," I add.
Dust collects on my shoulders. I pick at a hole in my cuff.
Conversation bores like a giant drill through the time-space
continuum as we travel unflinchingly towards our dessert.

The peppered chicken leads to a conversation on organic farming
and the bare-faced profiteering of Tesco.
"It's like Hitler," I add.
Dan argues that the only real alternative is battery farming,
which is a terrible way to die, crammed in like that.
"Like what Hitler did," I say.

My wife's friend Sandra explains how difficult it is
to find parking near her son's school
now that they have bought a Ford Galaxy.
"Fuck off back to Berlin," I say, putting down my fork.

Later, a pop group sings on the TV, neat as death.
My daughter appears to like the song.
"They are all Hitlers," I tell her. "And this song is Nazi Germany.
Each verse is an airbase, full of words
that will murder countless thousands once they get into the air."

People corner me in the pub, hands on hips,
trying to organise my hypothetical Hitlers.

I look at them and shake my head. I cannot tolerate
the purity they wish for.

"Little Hitlers," I call after them.
"I bet you wouldn't even go back in time and kill Hitler."
I pick up a copy of *Time Magazine*
and put my finger under the nose of Bill Gates.
"I would go back in time and kill Hitler," I say to my newsagent.

Outside the sky is Hitler. There is a cloud shaped like a black claw.
My sadness is the size of ten football pitches placed end to end,
as heavy as four double-decker buses.
I try to imagine something in this world that is still good and pure.

But then a dog with a moustache shuffles from the Woolwich.
A Belgian cinema, burning between my ears.

Experiment to Determine the Existence of Love

1.

Hypothesis

I suggest, were we to collide,
our compounds would bond like people do.
Then, once we cut away the control,
Love (L) would be evident —

for I strongly believe
our diagnostics
hide this volatile, stupefying element.

2.

Apparatus

Let us take a moon, hung low with commentary;
add our last reserves of serotonin.
Tan lines, mouthwash,
Charlie Parker, candle wax,
a bus pass, the Humber,
a few funny jpegs,
the way she lifts her leg into the waiting car,
two winters,
a faded poster of Lakshmi,
a walk-on cast of thousands,
and a minimum of two strong drinks
(but the goggles are optional, my sweetness).

3.

Diagram

The first draft is easy, public toilet stuff.
Arrows aimed at the obvious organs.
A quick sketch of the soul
that would make good John Venn blush.

Yet remember. This is not to scale.
Only functional processes and direction of data.
The flow charts stack up like decommissioned fridges,
the spaghetti programming of the heart.

Next the ghosts of each miscalculation,
each angle of vision, erased and redrawn,
all appear equal in your calipered eye,
indelible to the whiteout of time.

In its final state, the vortices spiral,
the subatomic data reflecting the whole.
The heart's fractal. The clinical vision.
The exploded body. The bloodless incision.

4.

Method

We begin with the control data:
tick-box stimuli we know we can trust.
Food we discuss,
and the state of the pavements.

By 2200hrs, advanced testing:
distrust of siblings and thoughts on suicide.
Attempts are made to touch knuckles.
Jazz is activated.

Then, from midnight onwards,
rogue elements are introduced.
Crepuscular statements and scratchy pencils
float out from behind each mirror.

The man at the table next to us
sings 'Yesterday' through a laryngophone.
A baby riding a smooth black pig
crashes through the mocked-up saloon.

Every ten minutes I visit the bathroom
and take a reading.

(Results as follows)

5.

Results

The night resembles a parabola curve,
curiosity rising with the humidity.

And when the thick, blood-red line
surfaces like an insane, contaminated salmon,
it survives ten minutes,
barely,
before floating back down below the zero.

6.

[Discussion]

A predominantly unsuccessful experiment
compared to solo results in the lab.
Prior research proved inadequate.
Alcohol safeguards were critically missing.

Lack of reaction can most probably be attributed
to persistent mispronunciation of *jalapeno*,
compounded by the glass eye of an unconvincing waiter
who pushed us beyond the expected anxiety buffer-zone.

All present were in agreement
that the pig should have been introduced earlier.

Without doubt, the experiment works in theory,
simply failing in transition from page to appliance.
Thus, we conclude, for now at least:
not a great day for Love,
but not a bad day for Science.

A Second Opinion

I told you what was in my heart.
You asked me to prove it, so
the next day
I brought round the x-ray.

This here, I said, tapping the acetate,
is the shadow cast by a sleepless dervish.
And these black spots across my left ventricle
are starlings above a collapsing pier.

This mass here
is a hospital lost in a power cut.
And this rather dark abrasion
is a dead fox overlapping an empty wardrobe.

Naturally, you were sceptical,
turning the sheet over and over,
holding it up to different lights,
calling in the neighbours for a second opinion.

My monochrome torso went up in the window
and we all stared at it from across the room,
as if looking at my very own exhumed grave—
a skeleton jammed in a chimney flume.

And I knew
that to the untrained eye,
the September evening in my chest looked mild.
But I trusted you, implicitly,
to take your coat with you
on the way out.

Last Dance

Some evenings, no words come easy.
She arrived late and looked in love.
(Love always looks like it wants something.)
She said she'd recently written a new dance.
It had taken her months and her feet were killing
her. She propped them against me and talked about

all the other things that were currently killing
her. Some of the things I already knew about;
Derek had already let slip the Big Something.
Um, I had said, and put on a record. We were in love,
once. Nowadays I don't like to dance.
She said, "Talking to you was never easy."

I think it depends on what you're talking about.
It's been over eight years since our last dance.
We laughed about it; how it was dark and easy,
like knocking a kid off a flyover. Killing
brain cells made us happy as ants. Something
to work towards, a job in the factory. "Did you love

me?" she said. Why? It's 4am and love
sounds like a crass pink inflatable. I'd prefer something
closer to "remember". It means more. After all, a dance
can fade in a decade too easy.
We smoked until the curtains gave up. She talked about
an old boyfriend in Derby who made a killing

selling black-market Ritalin, or something.
I agreed. All drugs lead to a killing.

E makes a mint, but it's bad for love.
You can't fuck, even if you forget about
what you've taken. Weed is good. Booze is too easy.
She asked me if I wanted to see her new dance.

As it turned out, it wasn't new or a dance.
Step by step it came back to us, easy.
"I can't sleep yet," she said. We knew that we were killing
time, as if at the end of it all there'd be something
to say about the thing that comes after love,
as if anybody knew what we were talking about.

These days I feel I'm always about to say something
on the after-hours of love. "Do you want to dance?"
OK, I said. Sleeping isn't easy when there are ants that need killing.

Poet in Residence for a Theatre in Liquidation

They say it knew it was dying:
a month, maybe more, but held it in;
kept the teeth at the front, kept polishing its glasses,
whistling Frank Loesser as the basement flooded.

Everything we do is a warning sign.

Only last week I stood in the office admonishing printers
and saw those filing cabinets teetering on the fire escape,
thinking, I wouldn't mind going that way myself.
Which was close to the truth, but not close enough.

Last night it was Aesop's fables.
Grandchildren waddled into their childhoods.
The counters smelt of branches and fixative.
Ten years later, someone is remembering this.

It happened at 22:34.
The manager stepped out to make a phone call.
That was all the time it needed.

Today the sun bounced from Bedford van bonnets;
I sat and watched as men in trim, blue uniforms
reassembled the theatre out on the lawn.
Summer began to feel like an elaborate set design.
Only movement broke the stillness.

Inside, the front-of-house pushed uncomfortably through the halls
as if the architecture had turned against them.

I found a rail of clothes,
accumulated over nine months of rushed get-outs:
a paisley waistcoat, a bike helmet, a tee-shirt that said DAN.
And I must admit
I wish I'd tried harder,
written more poems under the arches of that converted stable yard.
Not even good ones, that's not the point.

And not about the plays, either. More about those still
waiting for their cue, circulating in the wings, sick with prescience;
this tender world of transformation that can cut out at any time,
the fire exits leading us out under the shadow of the viaduct.

The applause of the trains above us. The moon.
Up in the cheap seats, just another retired actor.
Heaven's rig jabbing the Ouseburn River,
decontaminated, running backwards.

Return to a Compact Pastoral Settlement

Unemployed again, I spend my lunches packed into internet cafés, putting my CV into different fonts. I raise a carbo-shake to my lips. Today I'm occupied by a satellite image of a street I once lived on, a vast network of burnt-out microchips, a long string of probabilities, intersecting, veering off. A man mows his grass, and below, one worm becomes two, severed into parallel gardens.

I hang, parasitic, over the rooftops. What has changed since this image? Undoubtedly the grass is long again. Perhaps it has been re-cut.

This is a nice idea but lacks depth. Yet another private mess of perspective: something I am becoming accustomed to these days. Just as one day, walking under the fabulous parapets of Gambier Terrace, I saw my friend Dave walking towards me through the intermittent shade. "Great," I thought.

Yet as Dave approached I realised that it wasn't Dave. It was a young woman in a modest russet-coloured dress. "Great," I thought, but for different reasons.

This would have been enough, but as she passed, I looked up again, only to discover that she was actually an old Chinese man. I wanted to stop that man so badly. "My eyes just wrote their own poem," I would say.

In the end, I just told Dave, who was sitting in his garden and in no mood for poetry. The sun was too bright that day, and I was already thinking "The TV license, The TV license" and about how many things I would inevitably leave behind.

Ross Gordon Sutherland (anag.)

Let's honour grand dross:
grand holds on trousers.
Round arse holds strong.

Let's honour grand dross:
horrendous strong lads,
stoned horror, slugs and
dragons.
        Ruthless donor,
drug stasher, or London's
Godless horror?

          Nuts and
dross. Let's honour grand
gross sad hurt Londoner:

"Grr," sad Londoner shouts.